Lotería

Library of Congress Cataloging-in-Publication Data

Names: Rodríguez, Esteban, 1989- author.
Title: Lotería : poems / Esteban Rodríguez.
Other titles: Sabine series in literature.
Description: First edition. | Huntsville, Texas : TRP: The University Press
   of SHSU, [2023] | Series: The Sabine series in literature
Identifiers: LCCN 2023014054 (print) | LCCN 2023014055 (ebook) | ISBN
   9781680033229 (paperback) | ISBN 9781680033236 (ebook)
Subjects: LCSH: Mexican American families--Poetry. | Lotería
   (Game)--Poetry. | LCGFT: Poetry.
Classification: LCC PS3618.O35823 L68 2023 (print) | LCC PS3618.O35823
   (ebook) | DDC 811/.6--dc23/eng/20230407
LC record available at https://lccn.loc.gov/2023014054
LC ebook record available at https://lccn.loc.gov/2023014055

Cover design by Bradley Alan Ivey & Miranda Ramírez
Interior design by Miranda Ramírez

Printed and bound in the United States of America

Published by TRP: The University Press of SHSU
Huntsville, Texas 77341
texasreviewpress.org

Lotería

poems

Esteban Rodríguez

The Sabine Series in Literature

TRP: The University Press of SHSU
Huntsville, Texas

TABLE OF CONTENTS

2	El diablito	1
21	La mano	2
9	El barril	3
40	El alacrán	4
34	El soldado	5
42	La calavera	6
6	La sirena	7
12	El valiente	8
20	El pájaro	9
43	La campana	10
54	La rana	11
39	El nopal	12
45	El venado	13
52	La maceta	14
4	El cartrín	15
23	La luna	16
46	El Sol	17
27	El corazón	18
1	El gallo	23
22	La bota	24
36	El cazo	25
14	La muerte	26
32	El músico	27
25	El borracho	28
33	La araña	29
38	El Apache	30
30	El camarón	31
28	La sandía	32
31	Las jaras	33
24	El cotorro	34
18	El violoncello	35
7	La escalera	36
11	El melón	37
15	La pera	38

8   La botella   39
13 El gorrito   40
10 El árbol   45
53 El arpa   46
17 El bandolón   47
44 El cantarito   48
41 La rosa   49
26 El negrito   50
51 La palma   51
49 El pino   52
47 La corona   53
37 El mundo   54
29 El tambor   55
19 La garza   56
50 El pescado   57
5   El paraguas   58
16 La bandera   59
35 La estrella   60
3   La dama   61
48 La chalupa   62

Acknowledgments   65
About the Author   67

2 El diablito

When you imagine your father
in the desert, you also imagine the devil,
not the horned, goat-legged,
or personified snake version,
but the one that manifests as a small
shadowy figure, a trickster that follows
your father, places, when he's not looking,
rocks he stumbles over, or kilometers
of cactuses he must trudge through,
only to find, when he reaches the end,
mirages that make him believe
he is seeing cities, oil refineries,
floating islands that he can climb up
and rest on, forget how the devil pinches
his skin, or squeezes his throat,
or carves a fever across the back
of his neck, and how at night,
when your father thinks the stars
will ease the desert's uncertainty,
bangs on a drum just off in the distance,
as if to remind him that no matter
what corner of the earth he finds himself in,
his fate offers no moment of rest.

21 La mano

Without knowing why, your mother digs,
unaware and unconcerned with the cuts
on her palms, or with her nails peeling back,
or with the way her fingers begin to bend,
twist, resemble roots it appears she's unearthing
from the ground. And after digging for hours,
after enduring the gashes and punctures,
she finds a hand, severed cleanly at the wrist,
and adorned with rings that once had some
significance, but which now, as your mother
takes them off, have become objects
she can barter the desert with, one for shade,
one for water, one for a sign that the farther
she travels, and the more the sun boils her flesh,
the closer she is to something she can hold,
something that no longer feels out of her grasp.

9 El barril

There were nights when your father
drank alone in his truck—windows down,
radio on full blast. And when he was done
slurring *corridos* to the moon, he'd wander
to the yard, find one of the rusted barrels
he never used, and with night again
as his accomplice, start a fire, let it burn
brighter, brighter, while you, watching
from the corner of your window, imagined
it was the end of the world, that your father
was the last man, and because he knew nothing
would come after him, he grabbed whatever
was near, tossed it in—chunks of wood,
metal, brick, broken pieces of a playground set,
empty beer cans, trash stuffed in plastic bags.
And you wondered if he thought about
what he was throwing in, if he realized
all that he had hoarded over the years,
if he had ever considered cleaning it up,
or if he knew, every time he looked
at his unfinished projects in the yard,
that it wouldn't matter, because one day
he'd be here, ready, like any God,
to make what he owned disappear.

40 El alacrán

If you knew anything about deserts,
you knew there were scorpions.
So when one appeared in your yard,
standing where the crosshatched patches
of grass met the beginning of a field,
you thought you were in one, and your home
had been an oasis all along, or worse,
a mirage your decade on earth had been built
around. Either way, the scorpion wasn't
welcomed, and because it was moving closer,
because it was claiming land you didn't know
you felt so strongly about, you had to kill it,
had to find the nearest rock, and with anger
that made your body swell, had to slam it
on that scorpion, again and again,
until all you saw was black mush,
until you knew you were no longer a threat,
even to yourself.

34 El soldado

2007

March, but summer's heat
already occupies the air.
And in the middle of the yard
seated in the middle of your uncles,
aunts, your cousin smiles, babysits
a Bud Light because he can,
because nineteen is just a number,
and his deployment is near.
"Nineteen," your uncle jokes,
"and already you get to travel
the world," and because he knows
that that world is filled with promises
of IEDs, ambushes, shrapnel
and severed limbs, he adds,
"We're proud of you, mijo, proud
of what you're about to do."
But you wonder if you can be proud
of him too, if after accepting, without
question, what it means to invade
a country, you can accept he's a year
older than you, that your body
is no different than his, that in
a few months, while he's trudging
through rubble and sand, taking
position in a bombed-out house,
you'll be walking a new campus,
hopeful that at the end of each class,
you're one step closer to figuring
the world out.

42 La calavera

To get home from school,
you'd walk a field, and days after
the field was pummeled with rain,
you'd find scraps of wet cardboard,
soggy plastic bags, fragments
of toys you thought had no right
in such a place, but which you still
picked up, stuffed in your pocket,
hoped they could find a role
in the afterschool battles you waged.
And there was the day you found
what you assumed was a broken
bowl, bone-white and curved,
like ancient ceramic, and exciting
enough to show your mother,
who, when you said it looked like a skull,
snatched it from your hands,
and without looking at it, without
hinting on whether your guess was true,
stuffed it in a kitchen drawer,
then turned away and looked out
the window, as if she had just lost
something, as if she were remembering
someone she once knew.

6 La sirena

Though in the other room,
your aunts speak loud enough
for you to hear, and after chatting
about *novelas*, recipes, how hot summer
will be this year, the real *chisme*
begins, and they talk about your cousin
and her breasts, how large they've become,
how the good genes in the family
have finally kicked in. And in their back
and forth and back, some aunts are proud,
speak as if she has accomplished something
they have not, while others stay silent,
express with every passing minute
their discontent, that unhappiness
that when they were young they weren't
endowed with such a perfect chest.
And because your mother is one of them,
you remember how you walked in on her
once, bent over with nothing but underwear,
and how upon seeing her breasts—sagging,
wrinkled, more aged than you had expected—
you turned away, and have kept turning every time
she crosses her arms, or when her nightgown
reveals cleavage, or when on the beach
she adjusts her one piece, lets it snap—
again and again—against her ribs, as if she knows
that no matter how tight her suit fits,
she can make anything feel good on her skin.

12 El valiente

Sometimes, the story had your uncle
in the middle of the driveway, chest puffed,
knife in hand, cursing at the pair of men
who had just tried to break in his house.
And sometimes, the story had no men
at all, but instead a family of possums,
starving and rifling through the trash.
And in this version, your uncle wasn't
brandishing a knife, but a broom,
or at least a dustpan, and yes he cursed,
but it was near his door, protected
by the certainty of a porch light.
And when this is told by your aunt,
when she says she couldn't stop laughing
at him from the comfort of her couch,
you can't help but still think of him
as brave, that your uncle, having crossed
into this country in the dead of night,
knew what it felt like to face a darkness
that seemed to be whispering his name,
that tempted him to come closer,
that wanted his body to enter its folds,
and to believe that when he fully entered,
then and only then would he be safe.

20 El pájaro

And as he treks farther into this scalded
stretch of earth, weaving through clumps
of matted hide, heaps of broken bone,
your father spots a dead bird, believing,
at first, that it's nothing more than another
lifeless thing, until he comes closer, kneels
before it, and after wiping the sweat searing
his brow and eyelids, sees a key between
its ribs, small but shiny, and if not a sign,
your father thinks, then an opportunity,
one placed here by God or whatever god
demonstrates love with symbols and mysteries,
with the hope that as men like your father
seek a new land, a door will appear,
and they will no longer have to pray
for miracles, no longer beg for salvation
on their knees.

43 La campana

Decades later, and your mother is back
in Nayarit, only this time you are with her,
and from what you can tell there are no
remnants of helplessness, poverty,
of the reasons she migrated to a different
country. No, there is only a wedding,
and after the wedding, there is a reception,
a toast, drinks, and after there is you in a car
full of people and your drunk mother
sticking her head out the window, yelling,
laughing, cursing out the most random
of buildings, and making the car pull over
when she spots the church. And though
you feel embarrassed, though you want
to invent an excuse for her in your American
Spanish, you can't help but watch how she runs
toward it, finds the bell and pulls the rope
over and over again, causing dogs to bark,
lights to turn on, people to come to their doors.
And as the bell continues to ring, you know
that whether she's letting her hometown know
she's here or flaunting how easy it is now
to come and go, she has the attention she wants,
and even if no one listens, they will have to hear.

54 La rana

With the frog splayed before us,
the José whose parents are from Mexico
asks the José whose parents are from
Guatemala, "Isn't this the shit they eat
in your country?" And as he laughs
and slaps Guatemalan José on his back,
and Guatemalan José, to save as much face
as he can, forces a laugh just as loud,
I forget what step is next to dissect
this frog, think instead of my father again,
imagine that at some point of him crossing
the sun-seared edge of his land, he runs out
of food, and he must find, when night quits
its role as accomplice, something alive
enough to eat. And of course, in this version
of the story, he comes across a frog,
and with a rock or branch or the bottom
of his shoe, he kills and eats it raw,
never once questioning what he needs
to survive. And I wonder, if any part
of this is true, who wouldn't do the same,
if the parents of both José's had once
in their crossing moved through similar terrain,
and with nothing left, had consumed
whatever they could, confident that if they ate
insects, leaves, the dirt of the earth itself,
nothing about who they were would change.

39 El nopal

Like every dare that year,
you accepted, took a bite,
thought the nopal in your hands
tasted like cardboard and spinach.
And as you chewed through it,
wondered how you'd spend
your friend's money, you remembered
the story about the group of migrants,
how they were found in a shed,
how their bodies, rendered into headlines
and evidence, were, you imagined,
so pale and thin, because by the time
they'd arrived at that place, they,
perhaps like your parents, had done things
they never thought they'd do:
shit by boulders and bushes,
ignore the muffled screams at night,
forget again how many people
were in their group, and at some point
in their exodus, eat something
the desert had yet to devour,
a piece of carcass, an unknown plant,
whatever made them believe
that with one more bite,
there were sure to feel full.

45 El venado

Whether a dream or not,
you walk deeper into the woods,
lift the rifle you find in your hands
to your chest, and without knowing
what you're pointing at, fire
at the darkness, then listen to it moan.
And when you pull back the folds
of night, push past the labyrinth
of branches, you find a wounded deer,
kicking, struggling to get up,
and then, after you approach it,
kneel, turning so suddenly to ash,
so that all you're left with it your guilt,
is the knowledge that the unknown
made you react, and that you,
like a god, have become someone
who can choose to remember a death
no one else saw.

52 La maceta

When words no longer settled
an argument, your mother began
throwing objects at your father,
hand towels at first, then spoons
and spatulas, then the remote control,
until she arrived at the flowerpots,
the ones she had every intention
to use, but which, over the years,
as plant after plant died, she let fill
with spiderwebs, dust, with an extended
metaphor for her life—promising
but empty, intact but chipped,
nothing more than what could have been,
and what your mother figured,
in her attempt to make her point stick,
would show your father that he too
was to blame for this, that if he hadn't
been so silent, distant, had clocked in
when it was time to be a husband,
she wouldn't be throwing a *maceta*
at him, but instead be watered with care,
attention, with that touch that makes
even the most withered things bloom.

4 El cartrín

There was an uncle for everything:
dirty jokes, conspiracies, drunken
monologues at barbecues and birthday parties.
And there was Tío Roy, who, no matter
the gathering, dressed in bright polos,
seashell necklaces, bleached jeans
and boots made to walk Italian plazas.
Yes, this was the uncle who doused
his body in cologne, kept his shades on
at night, and who didn't care when his back
was turned and everyone—uncles, aunts,
cousins old enough to have earned an opinion—
gave a look that said how he dressed
was too much, that he wore his "happiness"
on his sleeve, not out of any sense to spread
his well-being, but out of his attempt to thrust
all of who he was in their faces, to make
his business theirs, to remind them,
despite their most silent objections,
that what makes anyone uncomfortable
never lives for long at a distance.

23 La luna

But again, how could you not personify it?
How could you watch the moon
from your backyard and not think that
it was watching back, that it was there
to witness events you can only imagine:
fire, bloodshed, the birth of new species,
civilizations. And in between the nuances
of life and death, there is your mother trying
to hide from the moon's glow, to use the darkness
as a shield, to avoid the way it follows her,
has betrayed its storybook innocence
to help the swarm of agents searching
for the group she was just in. And how could she,
at that moment, not believe the moon
was playing both sides, that it could be
a bystander one night, and the next
point its finger at these scattered women,
children, and men, some of whom are caught,
and who, when sitting against the agents'
trucks, stare up at the sky, convinced
even the moon is laughing at their luck.

46 El Sol

Like the moon, how could you not personify it?
How could you watch the sun from your front yard
and not think that it was spiteful, that it wanted,
since its genesis, to scald flesh, make bodies swell,
suffer. And every time you step out, every time
you put your hands on your knees, look for a shaded
spot, you think of your father in the desert, how he,
after losing the group he entered with, wanders
what he assumes is north, and with a cap and bandana
on his head, trudges on till he can't anymore,
till his body, seared in every synonym he can think of,
lays down to rest, and like you after a pickup game,
believes this is where he'll take his last breath.

27 El corazón

Your father wakes up, and among
the empty water bottles next to him,
among the backpacks and used bandages
scattered about, his finds his heart,
more cartoonish than he expected,
but large and beating and with an arrow
sticking out. Naturally, he picks it up,
watches the way it throbs, how the blood
it's slathered with drips like honey
to the ground, and how, even after he takes
the arrow out, he can't cram his heart
back into in his chest, looking—
as the desert heat thickens, and his flesh
drips off his bones—like a child hammering
a square peg into a round hole,
and hammering still even when his heart
is about to pop, even when he knows
it will never fit again.

1 El gallo

And when you got to high school,
you stopped giving them names,
no longer saw the chickens as Luz,
Maribel, Elena, Guadalupe, didn't try
to justify their open mouths for smiles,
their clucks for joy, their wing flapping
for how excited they were to see you again.
No, in fact you regretted that you ever
loved them in the first place, that at night
you would sneak one in, tuck her next to you
in bed, and in the morning, when no one
was looking, fed her pieces of your breakfast
from your hand, like she was a pet,
though you knew that she was anything but,
that sometimes, for reasons you didn't yet
understand, your father would go out
into the yard, and like a man surveying
what he knows can no longer live,
would grab one of your beloved chickens,
wring her neck, and with her limp body
in his hands, take her to a place beyond
the yard, where you prayed he'd pick
a spot you could easily find, walk to
when you felt alone, and reminisce.

22 La bota

At home, there was nothing your father
couldn't turn his work boots into—
a hammer for loose nails, a prop to even
stubborn tables and chairs, a weapon
to end the lives of anonymous insects.
And there were nights when he would sleepwalk,
and out in the yard with nothing but underwear
on, he'd smack together the bottoms of his boots,
as if there were spirits he had to ward off,
as if his past had taken on some once human form,
and to remind him that no one is ever free
of sin, made it its duty to stalk him at home.
And though it lasted no more than a few minutes,
and your mother would wake him up,
bring him back in, you figured that the boots
had done their job, that the reason he never used
sticks, pots or pans, or yelled at the top
of his lungs was because he wanted the spirit
to know exactly was who he was,
that he had every right to be at peace
on whatever ground he walked.

36 El cazo

Nuevo Progreso, 1997

At the end of the bridge, they sat,
women who for years had been scarred
by the sun and neglect, by the stares
of tourists, Winter Texans, or of those
who shared their last names, but because
of geography and fate, saw themselves
as different. And at your age, with your mother
by your side, and your grandmother,
who was from Mexico, leading the way,
you believed you were different too,
that the best you could have done was look
away, or, if that week you had saved
the money your mother gave you for school,
tossed a crumpled bill into a jar, saucepan, bowl,
into whatever made you feel that when you heard
the word *Gracias*, at least one woman's life
was about to change.

14 La muerte

Even after the whole school knew,
some still thought of her as *La muerte*,
callous of the cancer eating her organs,
of how much thinner her body
had become, of how sometimes,
in her attempt at normalcy,
she'd wear a hoodie over her wig.
And though you never told a joke,
you never stopped one either,
and now, looking back, wish
you had said these punchlines
weren't funny, or at least steered
the conversation elsewhere,
the way you steer it when small talk
begins to focus on your mother,
when you're asked how her chemo's
going, and you refuse to picture
the hair she's lost, the skin that's sagging,
or how she wobbles from her bedroom
to the couch, spends her day snoring,
only to wake up more confused
and lonely, even with you near,
and even when you put your arms
around her, and like the mother
that you never were, whisper
that there is nothing to fear.

32 El músico

On Congress and a street you still
don't know, you spot him, guitar in hand
but with no shoes, and by his feet,
an open case speckled with coins
and crumpled bills. And as he plays
a tune you think you've heard before,
you remember a story your father would tell,
how a man he once knew confessed
one tipsy night that when he was in the desert,
when he was at the point he believed his body
would soon stop moving, a figure with a small
guitar appeared, and while the group
he was with was sleeping, the figure knelt
by his side, strummed a few chords,
sung a few words, and then retreated
into that singed and swollen darkness.
And when your father would say
that the man said in that moment he felt "saved,"
you couldn't help but think the story
was really about him, that inventing someone
to describe his crossing would help him
understand if the lyrics were directions,
the chords a blessing, if the figure was his soul
and his soul was still wandering
the uncertainty of that desert.

25 El borracho

Each time, your father vowed to change,
said with body language alone
that the next time there was a birthday,
barbecue, the next time it was Friday night
and the week had tested how far
a middle age body could bend, twist,
move rebar and plywood for hours
on end, he'd down one less beer,
take one less shot that found its way
to his hands, pass on the *Jimador*,
micheladas, not be so quick to go
to the fridge, where he knew he'd find
something he had no intention to babysit.
I promise, his head tilt said. *Te prometo*,
his licked lips repeated. And you remember
how, before you even sipped your first drink,
you vowed to not be like him, to stop
and let water reanoint your lips. And yet...
and yet... twenty-one came, and you,
excited that it was Wednesday and 6th St.
was nearly empty, followed your friends,
said yes to everything thrust in your hands,
and knew, even as you gulped that blue drink
and passed into a newfound darkness,
you'd let these fires burn your throat again.

33 La araña

Like with the scorpion you once saw,
you think of territory, invasion, of the way
this spider, crawling confidently toward
your feet, wants to occupy your skin,
plant it's flag of fear across your toes
and ankles, incite a wave of goosebumps
that make your body violently shake,
and that prompt something you'll later
tell yourself—even though you were all alone,
and therefore absolved of claims you were a *sissy*—
was not a scream, but an *Oh God, Shit*, a grunt
that you could play off so as not to confess
to yourself that really you were scared,
that you weren't like your mother, who,
when at dinner a daddy long legs would appear,
would take her chancla off and smash it
right there on the table, or like your father,
who upon seeing a black widow once,
merely flicked it off his elbow, because he knew
it wouldn't harm him, that if he had one life to live,
he would be the one to say how it would end.

38 El Apache

Perhaps because he was silent.
Perhaps because he carried a small knife
by his pocket. Perhaps because his skin,
after decades of construction,
had darkened to the point of earning him
the nickname El Apache, which,
if this is what you had heard your aunts
and uncles call him, you figured
his coworkers did too, that when he
was on a worksite, they saw him
as the man who merely nodded
at instructions, stayed silent throughout
his shifts, and if he did have something
to say, if he was anything like he was
at home, he spoke in riddles, said,
in an English he was proud of,

If you can't listen to your feet,
        how can you listen to your heart;

A body is only as good as its spine;

When the wind whispers your name,
        whisper a secret back.

And the more phrases he uttered,
the more he was painted with such a broad
stroke, put into a box you try with each line
to get him out of, hoping the next time
you describe him, you will have painted
a portrait of someone else.

30 El camarón

Your father's plate arrived,
and you couldn't turn your eyes away,
couldn't fathom why the shrimp
was piled so high, that pieces
were falling off the edge.
And as your father dug in,
and more shrimp spilled,
you thought of that island
in the Mediterranean, the one
the news said was being met
with raft upon raft upon raft,
each packed with refugees,
so that when they reached the shore,
there'd be women and men falling
off the side, crawling toward safety
on their hands and knees.
But how many fell before?
Did they know their lives
would end in water? Did they
question God, lose faith in prayer?
And you wondered why exactly
you were thinking of them,
if it was right to compare
their struggle to your father
eating shrimp, or if really,
you were, in this roundabout way,
working through the meaning
of your father's journey: Mexico,
unemployment, the politics of *coyotes*,
or of a river whose mood can shift
so suddenly, and that when shifting,
growing stronger, made your father
believe he wouldn't reach the shore,
that fate had made sure
there was nowhere to go but under.

28 La sandía

Though unsure about the way fruit grew,
you knew your cousin wanted you to believe
that the watermelon seed would be in your belly
for months, that you, at such a young age,
would be no different than a pregnant woman,
large, bloated, ready for this thing to see
the light of day. And when you think of how
it would come out, you remember your mother's
stomach, how once when she lifted her shirt
to dry her hands, you saw the scar across it,
and before you could invent a story behind
what caused it—fall, knife fight, shrapnel—
she told you about her C-section, that you,
a stubborn little bastard, came out in a way
that made you special. And as your cousin laughed,
said he couldn't wait till he saw you fat,
you touched your belly, sure that if the seed grew
and the watermelon was ready, you'd cut open
your body to let it enter this world.

31 Las jaras

Where there was one broken arrow,
you thought there'd be another. And so
you dug holes across your backyard,
didn't stop until the ground looked
like it suffered a thousand tiny bombs.
And after, when you had to face
your mother's anger, had to listen
to your father's silent disappointment,
you imagined, even though this
was south Texas, tales of revolvers,
horses, knives and axes, and of course,
an onslaught of arrows. And perhaps
this one just missed sealing the fate
of a Cowboy. Or perhaps a Cowboy
broke the arrow piercing his chest,
and unable to believe such a thing
could bring about his end, damned God
and prayed that his life wasn't meaningless.
Or perhaps there was no violence at all,
but instead a kid who lived here
before you did, and who, to battle boredom,
chiseled an arrowhead out stone,
hoping that someone would create a story
around it, that its myth would make anyone
proud to call this place home.

24 El cotorro

Though half its feathers are gone,
it stares at you, repeats *What's your name?*
What's your name? And though
you remembered it being quite cool once,
feeling proud that this parrot was owned
by none other than your aunt, you now
look at it with pity, regret, with guilt
that prompts you to reach your fingers
in the cage, say *I'll get you out, I promise*
I'll get you out, knowing, however,
that your plan will live only in your head,
that when you pull your fingers back,
and hear your aunt from the other room
say to not get too close, you'll begin
to second guess, to imagine her anger,
screams, to believe your life is worth more
than one you could save.

18 El violoncello

In a ditch behind the school, you find a cello,
grimy, scratched, crosshatched with dead flies
and blades of wet grass. And as your friends
surround it, and one begins stomping on the neck—
a fuck you to every kid in band—you think
of who it belonged to, that it winding up here
was probably someone's idea of a prank.
And perhaps the owner is still looking for it,
wondering where such a large object
could be hidden. Or perhaps he or she
had tossed it here themselves, that they,
like all kids your age, had grown disillusioned
with what they once thought defined them.
And as you join your friends, rip out the strings,
kick the wood in, you imagine that this indeed
is your instrument, that if you are to become
someone different, you must destroy
what you thought you'd always love.

7 La escalera

Without saying a word, your father tells you
to climb the ladder, that if you are to be trusted
more around the house, you must do this task,
take the Christmas lights down. And so you climb,
make it to the roof when suddenly your father
yanks the ladder lose, lets it fall to the ground,
and with a silence bordering on laughter, walks
away, as if doing so will teach you a lesson,
will help you build character, make you a man.
And though you know you can let go, that the fall
will merely bruise your ankles, you find the strength
to pull yourself up, and once on the roof, you sit
and look at the yard, feeling like you just won a battle,
like the world was yours now, and yours alone.

11 El melón

Watermelons are too big, too suspicious,
your cousin said, so stick with a plain melon
instead. And once you cut it in half, use a spoon
to carve out a hole, you can mount it, practice
all you want, get good for your future girl.
And even if you suspected your cousin
had never done this, that he was and always been
full of shit, you can't help but look through
the groceries your mother brings home,
and as you search bag after bag after bag,
can't help but wonder what you'd do if there
was a melon, if you'd sneak it and a knife
to your room, if your body, desperate for knowledge,
would be ready to learn something new.

15 La pera

Of all things, it was the pear
that made her front tooth crack.
And as your mother screamed,
said *Puta madre, fuck, goddamn,*
you thought of how for years
it had slowly grown black,
had loosened from her gum,
had made you embarrassed
when she opened her mouth,
spoke, laughed. And you remembered
when you were near it, how you felt
you could smell the rot, knew exactly
what she had just eaten: tacos, fideo,
leftovers that were as hard as rocks.
And yet, despite all the candy,
pan dulce, the Sunday morning
Denny's Grand Slams, it was the pear
that did her in, that made her fall
at your feet, ask, as if you
had the answer, how something
this painful could come
from something so sweet.

8 La botella

You find one on the beach, label-less
and full of sand, more a ketchup bottle
than the bottle your uncles drink,
than the one your father, at birthdays
and Sunday gatherings, babysits, sips
in between jokes and drawn-out rants.
And as you pick up the bottle, pour out
the sand, you remember the night
your sleepwalking father made his way
to the porch, and after staring at the yard,
scratching his head, found a few bottles
resting by the steps, and without saying
a word, without noticing you were
for some reason there, grabbed the bottles
one by one, hurled them at the darkness,
as if he were trying to teach it a lesson,
or to at least let it know that when he
was done, walked back in, he always
had been and would be here.

13 El gorrito

If it was bright red, wrapped around
her head, if it was tied in a cute knot
below her chin, no doubt it would have
looked like a bonnet, and your mother
a different woman, not the figure
who used this faded rag to wipe off
an afternoon of sweat. No, she wouldn't
be cooking, cleaning, shuffling around
the kitchen, and she wouldn't be using
the rag one moment to clear her forehead
and the next to clean the counter,
and the next to go over to you and wipe
the chocolate from your lips, saying
you could be so messy sometimes,
but never asking why you were there,
what made you stand by the fridge
and think, as you watched her complete
her chores, that whatever your mother used,
wore, she would never be someone else.

10 El árbol

Before the river, a town,
and before the town, kilometers
of land filled with sagebrush,
carcasses, mirages scuttling
like rats. And though everything
looks a like prop, your father
trudges on, aware that the group
he entered this scene with
is no longer behind him,
that in the days to come
he will trek this stretch of earth
by himself, move from bush
to bush, rock to rock, until the sun,
having lashed a thousand fevers
on his skin, commands that his body
buckles, bends, moves beneath
the shade of the nearest tree,
where he will take off his backpack,
sit, sip water like it was the blood
of Christ, and wait till he can rise
again, till he doesn't feel,
every time he takes a step,
that some part of this world
is about to end.

53 El arpa

Like your father, your mother
never speaks of her crossing,
so you invent a narrative for her,
switch the river for a desert,
add a scene with carrion and carcasses,
with cactuses adorned with torn shirts,
jeans, bras and underwear, and on some,
black and white photographs of people
you mother once knew, but whose names
now, as she weaves farther in,
she can't remember, and which she forgets
about all together when she sees seated
at a distance a woman playing a harp.
And you could say she was naked,
or you could have her dressed in a white,
glowing garment, but you know
from what you know of your mother
that what this lady was or wasn't wearing
doesn't matter, just the melody coming
from her harp, the way the music
lulled her in, said this was where
she was supposed to be, and reassured her
that as she trudged on, imagined the land
on the other side, she knew she could believe
in something she didn't have to see.

17 El bandolón

In the back of your parents' closet,
it stands, dusty, dark, angled like a relic
against the wall. And you think that it must
be your mom's, that when she was young,
she took this instrument to parties,
and as the fun was winding down,
and everyone, either high or drunk,
began to lounge around, she'd pull it out,
play a song, let all who were listening
forget what it was they hated about the world.
Or maybe this instrument was your dad's,
and he brought it with him from his home
country. And though you know that the desert
wouldn't have allowed him to carry more
than a backpack, you imagined him with it,
that while his group had stopped to rest,
and the coyote, either distracted or past
the point of giving a shit, gave the group
his back, he'd play a song, sing about love,
despair, and, if the moment was right,
about the journey they were taking,
about the life they'd soon live on the other
side.

44 El cantarito

Like a centerpiece, it rested in the middle
of the table, sometimes filled, sometimes empty,
sometimes plagued by a season of dust and neglect.
And when the light made it seem important,
you thought not about the pitcher itself,
but about your grandmother's hands,
how old they looked against the glass,
how when you saw the veins you thought
of rivers, or of the ditches that filled with water
by the side of her house, or of comparisons
that didn't matter because you knew what seeing
her wrinkled skin meant, that when the body
reached this frail and shaking stage,
it was at the end, and lifting something,
anything was a testament of faith.

41 La rosa

It worked with your mother once,
so you thought it would work
with your father too, that when he
was given the rose, no matter
how shriveled and droopy it looked,
he would accept it, give you a hug,
say it was the sweetest thing
you'd ever done. But at eight,
what did you know of your father's
wants, of how much he valued things
for what they were, of how working
construction caused him to see the world
in numbers, measurements, in arranging
and rearranging what needed to fit,
and not seeing a wall, a roof, or building
as something more. No, you didn't know
he didn't think that deeply, that when you
presented him the rose, he would merely
nod his head, put it on the counter,
and leave it there till the meaning
you put behind it no longer mattered.

26 El negrito

Despite the world changing,
there were still those in your family
who called your cousin El negrito,
a name you heard argued years later was,
in its own way, a term of endearment,
but which when your uncles and aunts
used it, meant to show that your cousin's skin
was different, that he was darker than they were,
an anomaly they could use as a joke
as much as an insult. And once, at a barbecue,
when his own mother said it like his real name,
you watched how he squirmed in his chair,
saw a glimpse of anger shoot across his face,
which you thought he would turn, as soon
as he got home, into what you had heard
he once did when he was young,
into another scene where he takes off
all his clothes, turns the shower on,
and with a bar of soap tries to scrub his skin
off, hoping, even as the bleeding starts,
to reveal a new flesh, to peel back
what he was sure felt so wrong.

51 La palma

An oasis appears, and you walk toward it,
hoping, that like those narratives of your father
you invented, this is a godsend, that it is meant
as a break from your journey, a chance to strip
off your clothes, bathe in the water, and when
your body has again understood what it means
to heal, sit beneath a palm tree, and forget
the lives you lived before this one: the village
at the edge of a county; the droughts that swelled
the horizon; the awareness that the land
would remain unemployed, and that you,
being the oldest, would have to leave your family,
would have to cross deserts, mountains,
and when the clothes on your back were all
you had left, would still have to take another step,
accept a new faith of uncertainty.

49 El pino

But in this version, you come upon
a pine tree, and you find, nailed to its bark,
a black and white portrait of yourself,
one you don't remember taking,
and that looks, from the way you stared
at the camera indifferently, like you
were a prisoner, an enemy your enemy
captured, a soldier who after being processed,
found guilty, served as another example.
And as you try to place memories
to this image, you remember the photo
of your father you once saw in his wallet,
how much of an infant he was, how soft
his cheeks looked, how he smiled
because there seemed something to smile
about, and because nowhere in this moment
did the future have him packing his things,
leaving his village, or scrawling his boot prints
across the desert, like it was a language
only heaven could read, and that only heaven
had the answers to, could translate
the unknown into less of a mystery.

47 La corona

In your father's eyes you were basically
a man, and as a man he expected you bear
his laughter, jabs, that you withstand
the way he mocked your win, pretended
to walk onstage and put on a heavy crown.
Yes, you won the title of King, of being,
in the eyes of all your eighth-grade peers,
the most well-rounded and good-looking boy
that year. But you knew it was just a gala,
that the crown was plastic, cheap, that after
the excitement wore off, and a few days passed,
that whole night would no longer mean anything,
which you were okay with, but which your father
wasn't, perhaps because he felt you didn't deserve
this, or perhaps because he felt you did, that,
as he said before, the "good genes" that skipped
him were flourishing with you, and again
you were given what you didn't have to work for,
a life that was always yours to claim.

37 El mundo

Even in dreams, your father is working,
and in the version you'd been having for weeks,
he lifts a large replica of the world, places it
on his back, and because his body here defies
logic and physics, carries it up a hill, which,
after you wake up, you know is a metaphor
for twelve-hour shifts, for pounding nails
into wood, for sliding steel into slots again
and again, and for the days when his back
is shaped into a crooked punctuation,
and his feet, marking the floor into a hieroglyph,
have lost more of their purpose, becoming quiet
when he gets home, so that all you see of him
is not comparisons to language, but two
swollen limbs, a body reclined on a La-Z-Boy,
a father relieved to call this silence his own.

29 El tambor

Because you love Jumanji,
you make a drum of everything:
backseat, countertop, each and every
side of your knee. And when one day
you settle on the kitchen table,
you begin to drum in the middle
of dinner, slow at first, and then,
when the silence of no one telling
each other about their days becomes
unbearable, louder, louder,
so that your mother stares at you,
so that your father stands from his seat,
and without the sudden shift in moods
that define his nights of drinking,
places his hand on yours, and tells you
in English, *Stop it, please*, which you do,
and which prompts you to think
that at some point in his crossing,
he heard this exact same beat,
that as he moved closer to the river,
prayed his body would make it
through the baptism, it grew louder,
followed him, made sure when he
was no longer wet, he'd have no choice
but to remember that uncertainty
is always near.

19 La garza

Your aunt calls out the card,
and you don't think of a heron,
not even a bird, but instead
of your friends with the last name,
how they too would have thought
the same if they were in your place,
seated at the end of a table, flanked
by your uncles and aunts, convinced,
because the metaphor fits, that Lotería
was war, and that you were on
the front lines, putting beans on
your boards, while trying to translate
the cards beneath your breath:
alacrán-scorpion, *paraguas*- umbrella,
el mundo- the world. And *when la garza*
is called, you know, from the losses
you suffered before, that there is no time
to waste, that you must find that white
body, pink neck, and you must pretend,
even if you don't have it, that you do,
so that when your enemies look over,
try to see you what you're playing with,
they'll believe, if only for a second,
that you have the upper hand.

50 El pescado

Not your mother, but your father,
a small fish in the water. And when
the current is no longer personified,
and kilometers have become miles,
he washes up on shore, helpless at first,
until he gets his legs under him,
and like a new animal that begins
to walk the earth, staggers forward,
forward, moving with a lightness
he hasn't felt before, and that, days later,
when the sun has become black,
and the sky is flaked with ash,
takes him to another river, where
he knows he now has the right to enter,
to let his body unwind, float.

5 El paraguas

Then the desert begins playing games,
whispers different names in your father's ear:
Antonio, Martín, Edwin, José Luis.
And after it's uttered a thousand others,
after it tells him in so many languages
that the ground will soon consume his body,
it fills the horizon with mirages, prompts
your father to see highways, cities, lights
ripe with opportunity, promises, all of which
disappear when the desert wills a storm,
and then, as if to see him question his sanity
even more, places an umbrella near,
which of course your father reaches for,
but which the desert pulls away, farther,
farther, until it begins to rain, and all
your father can do is pray that when it floods,
the desert will show mercy, cast him
to a place his body can endure.

16 La bandera

Shirtless, he parades the median,
mutters to himself before he begins
shouting at the cars. And although
you want to hear everything he's saying,
although you want to connect his "hell,"
"please" and "fuck" into a larger meaning,
from where you stand you can only watch
as he pulls a flag from his backpack,
drapes it across his back, leaving you
and this midday traffic to watch him
wrapped in a tattered snake, eagle, cactus,
in the faded green, red, and white colors
you remember you once tried to lay claim to,
only it wasn't a flag, but a jersey for El Tri,
which your father, having grown up cheering
his beloved soccer team, stared at when he
saw you in it, and without thinking of it as homage,
began questioning why you were wearing it,
why you, who had never lived in Mexico,
who never watched *fútbol* in the first place,
would jump on the World Cup bandwagon
and cheer them on, and would, by screaming
after every goal, abandon the only country
you knew, the one that although exits
the tourney early, goes home still feeling
like they won.

35 La estrella

With his shirt unbuttoned, you see
the ink across your cousin's body,
the eagle, cactus, your aunt's name
and the name of an ex who was now
referred to as *puta*. And when you see
the stars on his shoulders, large
and vaguely three-dimensional,
you can't stop thinking how
they resemble *La estrella* in Lotería,
a card your cousin, this cousin
of all people, won with one night,
claiming some ten dollars in quarters,
nickels, dimes. And you remember
how clothed he was then, how the tattoos
he did have were hidden beneath
his white tee, so that not even his mother,
seated next to him, knew what he
was scarring on his chest, that it
was her name on his ribs—bold, cursive,
and perfect even if it wasn't complete.

3 La dama

Though your father opposed, believed
he alone should be the one to bring money
home, your mother accepted the job,
said that for the sake of who she was
she needed to do something that got her
out of the house, that yes, your father
was right, there'd be no cubicle, no
secretarial work, that her day indeed
would be spent cleaning other people's
homes, but at least she wouldn't feel
like she was stuck, wouldn't think that
she was bound to live her life only
within the same four walls. And though
you would have liked to see her in a jacket,
skirt, large briefcase in hand, there was
no way not to love her blue polo, khaki pants,
or the lunchbox packed with sandwiches
she spent the morning making, cutting
carefully in half.

48 La chalupa

For once, it's not about your mother,
father, not about deserts or exoduses
to other countries, but about you
and this canoe, about a river you find
yourself in, a moment where you stop
paddling, and in order to undergo
an "experience," look at the horizon,
let the eager sunlight bathe you,
let your skin, still scarred in old
adjectives, shine with new descriptions,
and let your body welcome whatever
emotion you think you'll soon feel,
because there is no one around you,
because history is raging somewhere
on shore, and because you accept,
for once, that whatever future lies ahead
was and will never be yours to control.

Acknowledgments

Many thanks to the editors of the following magazines and journals in which some of these poems first appeared:

Borderlands: Texas Poetry Review: "14 La Muerte"
The Common: "4 El catrín," "20 El pájaro," "34 El soldado," and "48 La chalupa"
Kissing Dynamite Poetry: "10 El árbol"
MiGoZine: "32 El músico," "37 El mundo," and "39 El nopal"
Negative Capability Press: "1 El gallo," "2 El diablito," and "22 La bota"
Nashville Review: "21 La mano"
Parentheses Journal: "12 El valiente"
Pigeonholes: "9 El barril"
Rouge Agent: "51 La palma"
Salamander: "40 El alacrán"
storySouth: "43 La campana" and "54 La rana"
Thrush Poetry Journal: "53 El arpa"
wildness: "37 El mundo" and "52 La maceta"

"22 La bota" was reprinted in the anthology Poetry Unbound: 50 Poems to Open Your World (W.W. Norton, 2022) by Pádraig Ó Tuama. Thank you to Pádraig for illuminating and appreciating such a poem.

"37 El mundo" was featured in American Life in Poetry. My gratitude to Kwame Dawes for showcasing and believing in my work.

Special thanks to John Hennessy. Your care and attention mean the world.

Thank you to Stephanie for being the first and best reader. Love you more than anything.

And thank you to my mother, father, and sister for their continued inspiration and support.

Esteban Rodríguez is the author of seven poetry collections, most recently *Limbolandia*, and the essay collection *Before the Earth Devours Us*. He is the Interviews Editor for the *EcoTheo Review*, Senior Book Reviews Editor for *Tupelo Quarterly*, and Associate Poetry Editor for *AGNI*. He lives with his family in south Texas.

The Sabine Series in Literature

Series Editor: J. Bruce Fuller

The Sabine Series in Literature highlights work by authors born in or working in Texas and/or Louisiana. There are no thematic restrictions; TRP seeks the best writing possible by authors from this unique region of the American South.

Books in this Series:

Cody Smith, *Gulf*

David Armand, *The Lord's Acre*

Ron Rozelle, *Leaving the Country of Sin*

Collier Brown, *Scrap Bones*

Esteban Rodríguez, *Lotería*